AF413112

GREATNESS AWAKENED

A Short Guide to Mastering Your Complex Brain and Unlocking Your Best SELF

Also by Roddy Carter

BodyWHealth: Journey to Abundance

Sunset Lessons: Reflections on Light and Love from the Darkest of Places

Fireside Wisdom: Conversations to Inspire Personal Mastery

The Problem With Anger: And How to Solve It

Becoming Unstoppable: Your Neurocentric Coaching Guide to Achieving Unstoppable Success

The Serpent Within: Navigating Fear to Restore Inner Harmony

Unstoppable Starts Here: A Short Guide to Mastering Your Brain and Unlocking Your Life

Unstoppable You Online Courses

Unstoppable You

Unstoppable You Business

Unleash Unstoppable

Unleash Success

Visit www.roddycarter.com for the full collection of Roddy's writing, including new and forthcoming titles.

GREATNESS AWAKENED

A Short Guide to Mastering Your Complex Brain and Unlocking Your Best SELF

Roddy Carter, MD

Aquila Life Science Press
La Jolla, California

FIRST AQUILA LIFE SCIENCE PRESS EDITION, FEBRUARY 2026
Published by Aquila Life Science, LLC, La Jolla, CA

GREATNESS AWAKENED.

Copyright © 2026 by Aquila Life Science, LLC.
Editing and book design by Sarah Dawson, WordPlay Editing.

All rights reserved.

No part of this publication may be reproduced, stored in a
retrieval system, or transmitted in any form or by any means,
electronic, mechanical, photocopying, recording, scanning,
or otherwise, except as permitted under Section 107 or
108 of the 1976 United States Copyright Act, without the
prior written permission of the Publisher. Any request to the
Publisher for permission should be sent to Aquila Life Science,
LLC, at connect@aquilalifescience.com.

Limit of Liability/Disclaimer of Warranty: While the publisher
and author have used their best effort in preparing this book,
they make no representations or warranties with respect to
the accuracy or completeness of the contents of this book and
specifically disclaim any implied warranties of merchantability
or fitness for a particular purpose. No warranty may be
created or extended by sales representatives or written
sales materials. Some materials included with standard print
versions of this book may not be included in the e-book or
audiobook version.

ISBN: 979-8-9990257-4-6

Printed in the United States of America

*For every soul who has felt the inner chorus,
the many voices, the pushes and pulls,
and wondered which one was truly yours.*

*This book is your invitation,
not to become someone new,
but to begin the careful journey
of awakening the greatness
rising deep within.*

Introduction

The Angel in the Marble

We've been told a lie.

We've been told that greatness is something we must chase: something out there waiting beyond the next milestone, the next win, or the next reinvention. We've been trained to believe that, if we just perform better, polish more perfectly, or hustle harder, we'll finally be worthy.

But what if this is wrong?

What if greatness isn't earned at all?

What if greatness is something already present within us, waiting not to be built but embraced?

The artist Michelangelo, when asked how he created one of his most famous statues, is said to have answered:

> "I saw the angel in the marble
> and carved until I set him free."

He didn't invent the angel. He didn't construct it from scratch. He simply revealed what was already there, hidden within the marble slab.

More than a profession, my work as an executive coach and author is a privilege. It is a gift to walk beside people as they awaken to the truth of their inner greatness.

You are the marble. And your greatness is already within you, waiting to emerge.

Chapter 1

Why We Forget

If it is true that we are already great, then why don't we feel that way? Why do so many smart, accomplished, hardworking people feel like imposters in their own lives?

The answer lies in their magnificent *Polymorphic Mind.*

Far from the unified leader you might have always envisioned, your mind is composed of many sub-personalities, each shaped by your early experiences. You are not one mind, but many. You are a mosaic of inner voices, each forged by your nervous system in response to an early experience.

These sub-personalities (that I refer to as *Parts*) are brilliant protectors programmed in the biological depths of your brain. They help you fit in, stay safe, be accepted, and, above all, survive.

These Parts may also be referred to as *ego contructs*, and collectively, they make up your complex psyche.

At the center of your algorithm-based psyche—beneath the fear and beyond the striving—lives your *Authentic SELF.*

Unlike your reactive Parts, this SELF is steady, compassionate, and wise. It doesn't need applause to know it's valuable. It doesn't need perfection to know it's worthy.

Your greatness lives in that SELF. Quiet. Waiting. Unafraid.

It has always been with you. In fact, it *is* you.

But over time, your devoted, survival-based sub-personalities begin to hide your true SELF within layers of caution—clinging, resisting, and deploying other complex strategies like perfectionism and people-pleasing.

In other words, these protective algorithms guard your true SELF from harm but inadvertently obscure your natural brilliance along the way.

You learn to *become* lovable rather than remembering that you *are* loved. You strive to *earn* worthiness instead of knowing that you *are* worthy.

These Parts aren't enemies. They're loyal bodyguards. But in guarding you, they bury you.

Most of us live under the authority of our sub-personalities—especially the striving ones.

We think, *If I just get this right...* or *If I can be better...* or *If I earn enough, do enough, prove enough... then I will be safe, happy, loved, respected, and fulfilled.*

But you must remember that these are not your authentic voice but rather the voices of your ego, propagated by deep brain algorithms. They mean well, but they've forgotten that you already are enough.

And so, your greatness is not lost. It is simply hidden.

When we awaken to our greatness, we stop asking, *What must I do to be enough?* And we start asking, *What can I release, so that my enough-ness can be seen?*

Awakening is not an act of invention; it is the practice of remembering, of carving away what is not true so that what *is* true can surface and breathe again.

You don't have to become someone new. You simply have to uncover the truth that's always been yours.

Your greatness is not a distant goal; it is your inheritance. It is not a reward but a deeper inner truth.

This is your greatness, awakened.

Your Practice

Here is a quiet place to begin:

- *Close your eyes. Find a comfortable position. Let your breath slow. Notice your body settling into stillness.*

- *Set aside the impulse to improve, fix, or prove anything. This is not a moment for performance; it's a moment for permission. If your mind races to "do it right," simply notice that voice. Thank it quietly, and return to stillness.*

- *Ask yourself gently,* What if I've been great all along? What if I've already been enough, even on my hardest days? What if my striving has been evidence of my greatness, not proof of its absence? What if nothing has ever been missing from me—only hidden? What if the voice I've called doubt is simply my greatness asking to be heard differently?

  Let the questions land softly, without forcing an answer. Imagine them *dropping like pebbles into a deep lake. Just observe the ripples.*

- *Listen—not for a shout, but for a whisper.*

  The answer may arrive as a word, a feeling, a memory, or simply a sense of calm. You might hear a voice that says, "You are enough." Or perhaps you'll feel warmth in your chest or see an image of yourself at peace.

  You might also hear silence. That's okay. In silence, your nervous system is learning that stillness is safe.

If nothing arises, know that you've already begun. The marble must first be touched before it yields its angel. With each repetition, you are teaching your brain that it no longer needs to strive for worthiness— because your worthiness has always been there.

Use these pages to record your reflections.

Chapter 2

From Fate to Freedom

Most of us are not living freely. We are living on autopilot.

This is not because we are lazy or stupid but rather because much of our behavior is driven by forces we cannot see: ancient internal strategies embedded so deeply in our neural wiring that we mistake them for our primary personality.

Carl Jung identified this with startling clarity:

"Until you make the unconscious conscious,

it will direct your life and you will call it fate."

Let's return to the Polymorphic Mind and your internal boardroom of protective sub-personalities.

Each of these Parts developed in response to your personal experience, many during your earliest years, when your brain was rapidly adapting to your environment. These brain-based algorithms learned what earned love, what triggered danger, and what kept you safe.

Then, in service of survival, they automated your life.

The result? You move through the world reacting in familiar ways, telling familiar stories, and believing familiar truths, all shaped by unconscious neural pathways that were once adaptive but may no longer serve your best interests.

And because these programs are hidden, you call it fate: "This is just how I am." "This always happens to me." "No matter what I do, I end up back here."

These behaviors are not fate. They are neurobiological computational loops.

You see, your brain is highly efficient.

Once it detects a recurring thought pattern, especially one that serves survival, it conserves energy by running it automatically. It drops it from consciousness into the deep unconscious. This is the function of the *default mode network (DMN)* and other predictive processing systems in the brain.

But what begins as efficiency can become entrapment.

Unless we pause to examine which algorithms are leading our lives, we are not living from awareness or freedom. We are living from programmed reactivity.

Understanding this, you now have the opportunity to take the next deliberate step on the journey to greatness: observation without fusion.

Notice, without judgment, when you are reacting from an unconscious place.

Gently ask, "Who is speaking right now?" or "What are they trying to protect?" or "Is this pattern still serving me?"

This is not about blame. It is about awareness, because only what is seen can be softened. And only what is understood can be rewired.

Fate is not fixed. Your current state is the result of an ongoing script written by overlooked and forgotten inner voices, acting out of love but locked in time.

You have the power to revise this script. You have the freedom to lead from your Authentic SELF.

Let this be your next awakening: a gentle rebellion against automation and a quiet return to conscious choice.

You are not your brain. You are not your programming or your algorithms.

You are the one who can see them—and the one who is free to choose.

This is your greatness, awakened.

Your Practice

Try this:

- *Think of a moment when something has triggered you: a disappointment, a fear, a familiar tension.*

- *Pause.*

- *Ask, Is this a conscious reaction? Or is it a protective reflex?*

- *Identify the sub-personality that has been activated, if you can. Just noticing and naming it loosens its grip. To help, ask yourself:*

Is this my Perfectionist, desperate to get it right?

Is this my Pleaser, afraid that disapproval means danger?

Is this my Controller, tightening its hold to prevent loss or chaos?

Is this my Critic, speaking harshly to keep me safe from shame?

Is this my Fixer, rushing to solve what might simply need compassion?

Is this my Escapist, seeking distraction or withdrawal to avoid pain?

Is this my Achiever, striving to prove worthiness once again?

Each of these Parts has a purpose. Each once served you well. But their reflexes may no longer match the world you now inhabit.

If you repeat this process regularly, you will start to see the automation. And in time, you will awaken from it.

This is the slow and steady work of awakening to the truth of your greatness—not by force or performance, but by bringing the unconscious into the light.

Use these pages to record your reflections.

Chapter 3

Truth, Not Performance

Somewhere along the way, many of us lose track of who we are.

This is not because we are careless but because we are care*ful*. We adapt. We perform. We become who we think we have to be, believing it will keep us loved, safe, and successful.

And it works…until it doesn't.

The performance earns praise, but not peace. It builds a life, but not freedom. It protects us and drives our early success, but it cost us ourselves.

This is where many people arrive: successful, respected, functional…and quietly unsure who they truly are underneath it all.

So, if you're at this point of deep (and often hidden) inner uncertainty, don't give up. May the words of Carl Jung, one of the founding voices of soul science, inspire you to keep growing:

"The privilege of a lifetime is
to become who you truly are."

The journey of becoming is not a reinvention. It's a realignment.

You are not here to manufacture a new identity. You are here to rediscover your original one: the Authentic SELF deep within, buried but never broken.

And I believe there is a simple path to become who you are.

But it is not easy.

Because to become who you truly are, you must first recognize, and then gently disidentify from, who *you are not*. It isn't possible to simply carve away and discard the ego; its algorithms are woven into the neurobiology of your magnificent brain. But you can loosen its grip on you. And this is the pathway to doing so.

Through the *Polymorphic Mind Model*, you've come to see that your inner world is not a single voice but a rich mosaic of voices, each with its own needs, fears, and protective patterns. These algorithm-based Parts have been at work for decades, loyally shaping your behavior to keep you safe, win approval, or avoid pain. They have been your drivers and your protective masks.

Because many of these voices emerged early in your life—long before you had the perspective to understand them—you assumed they were your own. In fact, you first heard them during the very years you were forming a separate identity from your parents and family. You knew what your parents' voices sounded like, and the voices in your head didn't sound like them. So, you drew the only conclusion available at the time: They must be you.

No wonder you still think *they* are you. This deep misidentification is natural.

And yet, it is precisely this misidentification that obscures your Authentic SELF. These Parts are not you. They are expressions of past survival strategies captured in neurobiological algorithms, not reflections of your deepest, enduring truth.

Your brain has coded your false identity in malleable, plastic structures, fluid circuits shaped by experience. Frequent use has cemented them.

Each time you repeat a thought or behavior, those identity circuits strengthen. This is how your sub-personalities become so deeply entrenched and so convincing; they've been rehearsed for years. And they react faster than you can think.

But, luckily, this neuroplasticity also means that, when you confront your protective patterns with awareness, compassion, and choice, you can literally reshape your sense of self. With time, disuse weakens the biologic circuits that sustain these outdated algorithms, and they begin to loosen their steely grip on your life.

This is not a vague, ungrounded hope. It is neurobiological reality.

When the brain feels safe, it opens to scrutiny. When it is seen without shame, it opens to rewiring.

Your greatness does not live in your performance. It lives in your underlying truth. It emerges when your protective Parts trust you enough to relax their roles, ceding authority back to your original Authentic SELF. To become who you truly are, you must release who you once needed to be.

Let this be your next awakening: a bold step away from the performance and toward the truth.

This is your greatness, awakened.

Your Practice

Try this:

- *Notice moments when you feel pressure to perform, please, or perfect.*

- *Pause.*

- *Ask, What Part of me is leading here?*

  Is this my Performer, working tirelessly to earn love or approval?

  Is this my Competitor, driven to prove I'm the best...or at least not the worst?

  Is this my Expert, afraid to make a mistake or be seen as less than competent?

  Is this my Caretaker, believing that peace depends on keeping everyone else happy?

  Is this my Diplomat, fastidiously managing every little word to avoid conflict?

Is this my Solider, powering through exhaustion to maintain control?

Is this my Invisible One, staying small so that no one will judge or reject me?

- *Then, ask gently,* What would my Authentic SELF do if it felt safe to lead in this moment?

You may not always know the answer, but the question itself is a shift. It reminds the nervous system that a different path is possible.

Use these pages to record your reflections.

Chapter 4

Healing, Not Hiding

Many of us stop working, and hence growing, when it hurts. When we do this, we cannot awaken our greatness.

If you observe closely, you will discover an interesting irony: Some wounds never stop aching. Some pain appears to persist, echoing stubbornly, despite your best efforts to avoid it. This happens not because we are broken but because we are brilliant.

The human brain remembers. Painful memories are deeply encoded within the very algorithms that have kept you safe and enabled your survival. They live within the code that drives your protective sub-personalities.

And until those wounds are seen, softened, and integrated, they will shape your life from the shadows, leaving you to wonder why success doesn't feel like peace, or why love still feels risky, or why joy sometimes slips away as soon as it arrives.

But here's the deeper truth: Your pain is not a flaw. It's a signal.

It's not the end of your greatness; it's the pathway to it. As the renowned mystic and poet Rumi wrote:

"The wound is the place where
the light enters you."

Every automatic reaction has a reason. Every sabotaging inner voice has a story encoded deep within its biologic programing.

And most of those stories include some kind of wound: a moment when something felt too much, or not enough. A moment when the world taught you that love was conditional or that vulnerability was unsafe.

Your mind didn't make that up. It simply recorded it.

And your loyal and vigilant brain built neural scaffolding around that wound to keep it shielded.

It did it to protect you. But in doing so, it also walled off and obscured your deepest wisdom.

You see, in the Polymorphic Mind, your pain isn't just a memory; it's embodied as a sub-personality.

A young one. A silent one. A scared or angry one.

It may only speak in defensiveness, withdrawal, perfectionism, or fear. It may not even speak in words, just in bodily tension, visceral emotion, or relational sabotage.

But it is there.

And it's not waiting to be punished. It's waiting to be held—with compassion and respect.

Now, here's the paradox: The places we've hidden from are often the very places our strength is waiting to be reclaimed.

When a wound is left unprocessed, the amygdala and other limbic structures tag it with danger, and your brain builds detours around it to avoid emotional pain.

But this unconscious rerouting becomes limiting.

True healing begins when the wound is gently revisited with safety and compassion. This signals to the nervous system that the threat has passed. Through the calm lens of your prefrontal cortex, you reappraise the event, the resultant protective algorithm, and its meaning. This is when neuroplasticity rewires old pain into present wisdom.

Healing, in this way, is not erasure. It's reintegration.

There is wisdom in your wounds, not because the pain was right or fair but because you survived it. And in surviving, your brain built reactive algorithms that were strong, loyal, and protective.

But, until now, they have led you.

And now it's time for *you* to lead them.

It's time to return to those old, painful places, not to get lost in the hopelessness or helplessness in which they were formed but to reveal your truth.

Because your greatness doesn't lie in the untouched gaps. It lies hidden behind the protective structures that guard these wounds.

Let this be your next awakening: not to hide your wounds but to heal through them.

This is your greatness, awakened.

Your Practice

Try this:

- *Notice moments that evoke a strong emotional reaction, especially ones that feel out of proportion to the situation. It might be a sharp tone from a colleague, a partner's silence, or an unexpected setback. Notice what rises in you: anger, shame, fear, or withdrawal.*

- *Pause. Take one slow breath. Soften your shoulders. Feel your feet on the floor. This small pause signals to your brain that you are safe enough to observe, rather than react.*

- *Ask, What Part of me might be hurting, or even hiding, behind this reaction? If it helps, imagine turning inward as if you were meeting an old friend. Consider:*

  Is this my Timid One, afraid of being unseen or forgotten?

  Is this my Protector, stepping in with anger to shield that hurt?

Is this my Achiever, panicking because failure feels unsafe?

Is this my Lone Wolf, convinced it's easier not to need anyone?

Is this my Gratifier, fearing that love will be withdrawn?

- *Without judgment, turn toward it and ask, What did you need that you never got?*

  Perhaps it's reassurance, protection, kindness, or simply permission to rest. Listen for whatever arises: words, sensations, or silence. Each response is valid.

  If nothing comes, that's perfectly okay. Silence simply means this Part isn't ready to speak yet. The act of turning toward it, rather than away, is already healing.

Remember, the goal isn't to fix; it's to listen. Listening tells your nervous system, I am safe enough to care for what once scared me.

That's where healing begins.

Use these pages to record your reflections.

Chapter 5

Peace, Not Perfection

At some point on this journey, after you've remembered your worth, reclaimed your freedom, embodied your truth, and embraced your inner power, a new question arises:

How do I live like this every day?

How do I lead a busy, complex life—relationships, work, family, dreams—and achieve success, not from striving but from stillness? Not from perfection but from peace?

This is the quiet culmination of greatness awakened: leading from the Authentic SELF. Not occasionally. Not when the stars align. But as a steady, internal presence.

And make no mistake, this peace is not passive. It is *embodied power.*

It is the natural authority of someone who knows who they are and no longer needs to prove it.

For many of us, performance and perfection have been lifelong shields. We strive. We polish. And then we push even harder, hoping, often unconsciously, that perfection will protect us from pain, judgment, or rejection.

But perfectionism, and people pleasing, and work enslavement are never about excellence. They're about control. They are usually led by inner voices driven by fear—afraid that, without perfection or affirmation or control, we won't be enough.

These voices are earnest, loyal, and tireless.

In your early life, before you had the strength or perspective to protect yourself, they stepped in to shield you from harm. They became your default leaders, reacting quickly to keep you safe.

But you are no longer that vulnerable child. You now have the wisdom, strength, and presence to care for yourself. Those protective sub-personalities can now rest, because *you* are ready to lead.

In the Polymorphic Mind, peace doesn't arise from silence or lack of conflict; it emerges when your inner voices trust your Authentic SELF enough to step back. And then, finally, you will recognize the state described by Chinese philosopher Lao Tzu, who observed:

> "When I let go of what I am,
> I become what I might be."

You'll recognize this state not by perfection but by presence and not by control but by coherence.

When the Authentic SELF leads, certain qualities begin to appear—not as performances but as expressions of your truest nature: A grounded clarity and calm. Gentle strength. Honest self-trust. Open-hearted and courageous curiosity. Wise discernment. Deep compassion. Creative flow. Emotional spaciousness. Quiet confidence. An unshakable sense of belonging.

This is not a static state. It is living leadership, a gentle but firm authority, like a seasoned champion striding through life with both humility and conviction.

These are not traits to master. They are innate powers to unlock. They become the signals that your true leadership is back in the ascendancy.

Neuroscience confirms this state. When the SELF leads, the prefrontal cortex is online, integrating memory, regulating emotion, and directing thoughtful action.

By contrast, traits like perfectionism and people-pleasing are often fueled by hyperactivity in the anterior cingulate cortex and the amygdala, regions tied to error detection and fear.

When you drop the protective scripts, the brain moves from hypervigilance to coherence. Cortisol and other stress hormones decrease. Heart rate variability improves. The DMN relaxes. And your system returns to its natural intelligence.

Peace isn't the reward for getting it right. It's the result of choosing what's true.

Previous, effortful approaches may have impressed the world, but they rarely satisfy the soul. Peace, on the other hand, allows you to lead, to love, and to live from the deepest part of who you are.

Let this be your final awakening: not to strive, but to settle. Not to prove, but to embody. Not to polish, but to reveal your natural brilliance.

This is your greatness, awakened.

Your Practice

Try this:

- *As you live forward with this new knowledge, notice moments where you feel pressured to get it right.*

- *Pause.*

- *Ask, What options are at my disposal in this moment? And, Will I choose the path of peace or the ingrained strategies recommended by my protective Parts?*

- *Then ask, What would my Authentic SELF choose to do right now—not to impress but to lead, effortlessly?*

It might be a small act: a breath, a boundary, a kind "no," or a brave "yes." Let it come from calm, not compulsion.

Use these pages to record your reflections.

54

Conclusion

Your Greatness, Awakened

Awakening your greatness is not about reinventing yourself or pretending to be someone you're not.

It's about moving from the unconscious reactivity of ego-led living to the calm efficacy, joy, and peace of a life led by your Authentic SELF.

In reading this little book, you have taken a meaningful first step in awakening the greatness that lies within you.

Along the way, I hope you've begun to notice the voices of your unique sub-personalities, encoded in neurobiological algorithms deep within your magnificent brain.

You've learned how they developed to protect you and have remained your most devoted servants— even though their approaches may no longer serve you well.

You've learned how these protective Parts build walls around your deep Authentic SELF, diluting and inhibiting your natural power.

Most importantly, you've started noticing when these Parts take over, and hopefully you have begun to gently redirect them.

That alone is transformational, and I hope that you've begun to appreciate your deep authentic power.

But while this book has given you key insights and practices, it's just the beginning of what's possible.

My broader collection of written works, my workshops, and my personalized coaching are designed to take you deeper, guiding you through additional steps that will bring your learning to life, identifying your unique neurobiological profile and unlocking your fullest potential.

I invite you to explore my work more closely as your next step to dramatic and enduring transformation.

In particular, I invite you to explore the possibility of working directly with me in a profoundly impactful immersion coaching experience. Together, we'll thoroughly explore and define your unique mosaic of neuroprotective adaptations that are limiting your success.

True transformation isn't a one-time shift. It's a process—a return, again and again, to the deepest part of you, that's wise, courageous, and whole. This is the road to greatness.

In my experience, those who step forward quickly are rewarded with rapid growth and enduring results. Those who hesitate continue to suffer the pain of mediocrity and the frustration of sub-optimization.

So let's keep going, right away.

Scan the QR code below or visit me at roddycarter. com to continue awakening your greatness.

The next chapter of your journey is within your reach—and I'd be honored to walk it with you.

If this book resonated with you, I'd be honored if you'd leave a review on the site where you purchased it...your voice helps others find it.

www.ingramcontent.com/pod-product-compliance
Lightning Source LLC
Chambersburg PA
CBHW040808150726
48196CB00058B/1462